TIME TRAVEL GUIDES

THE ISLAMIC EMPIRES

Louise and Richard Spilsbury

Raintree

Chicago, Illinois

Designed by Clare Nicholas
Illustrations by Peter Bull
Printed and bound in China by Leo
    Paper Group

12 11 10 09 08
10 9 8 7 6 5 4 3 2 1

Library of Congress Cataloging-in-Publication Data
Spilsbury, Louise.
  The Islamic Empires / Louise and Richard Spilsbury.
    p. cm. – (Time travel guide)
  Includes bibliographical references and index.
  ISBN 978-1-4109-2911-2 (library binding - hardcover)
  – ISBN 978-1-4109-2917-4 (pbk.)
  1. Islamic Empire–Juvenile literature. I. Spilsbury,
Richard. II. Title.
  DS38.3.S65 2007
  909'.1–dc22
                        2007006035

Acknowledgments
The publishers would like to thank the following for
permission to reproduce photographs:
AKG p. **44** (Jean-Louis Nou); Art Archive pp. **13** (British
Library), **15** (Topkapi Museum, Istanbul/ Dagli Orti), **18**
(National Library, Cairo/Dagli Orti), **20** (Dagli Orti), **21**
(Museo Correr, Venice, Italy/Dagli Orti), **25** (National
Museum, Damascus, Syria/Dagli Orti), **30** (Dagli Orti),
40 (Bodleian Library, Oxford), **42** (Victoria and Albert
Museum, London/Sally Chappell), **49** (British Library),
51 (National Library, Cairo/Dagli Orti); Bridgeman
Art Library pp. **8** (Egyptian National Library, Cairo), **27**
(Bibliothèque Nationale, Paris, France), **36** (Reza Abbasi
Museum, Tehran, Iran), **53** (Museo Correr, Venice, Italy/
Giraudon); Corbis pp. **12** (Steve Raymer), **16/17** (Firefly
Productions), **26** (Ed Kashi), **28/29** (Shepard Sherbell),
35 (Free Agents Limited), **43** (Kazuyoshi Nomachi/
Bettmann), **45** (Archivo Iconografico, S.A.), **46/47** (Nik
Wheeler), **54/55**; iStockphoto pp. **6/7** (Paul Fisher), **10**
(John Woodworth), **11** (Jan Rihak), **19** (Jane Norton), **24**
(Matej Michelizza), **33** (Simon Gurney), **37** (Christine
Rondeau), **38/39** (Jim Lopes), **59** (Damir Cudic); Werner
Forman p. **41** (Werner Forman Archive/Alhambra
Museum, Granada).

Background cover photograph of the Dome of the Rock,
Jerusalem, reproduced with permission of Brand X
Pictures. Inset photograph of gold deer from Cordoba
reproduced with permission of Corbis. Inset photograph
of tile reproduced with permission of the Bridgeman
Art Library.

The publishers would like to thank Professor Timothy
Insoll for his assistance in the preparation of this book.

Every effort has been made to contact copyright holders
of any material reproduced in this book. Any omissions
will be rectified in subsequent printings if notice is given
to the publishers.

Disclaimer
All the Internet addresses (URLs) given in this book were
valid at the time of going to press. However, due to the
dynamic nature of the Internet, some addresses may
have changed, or sites may have changed or ceased to
exist since publication. While the author and publishers
regret any inconvenience this may cause readers, no
responsibility for any such changes can be accepted by
either the author or the publishers.

CONTENTS

Words that appear in the text in bold, **like this**, are explained in the glossary.

N
W E
S

Vienna

Constantinople
(Istanbul)

•Rome

SPAIN

Cordoba

Granada

SICILY

ATLANTIC
OCEAN

TUNISIA

MEDITERRANEA

MOROCCO

Cairo

EGYPT

AFRICA

SONGHAI

Dome of the Rock

MALI

Area ruled by the Islamic Empires by 750

Area ruled by the Islamic Empires by 1250

Great Mosque
Samarra

BLACK SEA

CASPIAN SEA

MAP OF THE ISLAMIC EMPIRES

Samarkand

SYRIA

TIGRIS

EUPHRATES

SEA

Samarra

Isfahan

Damascus

Jerusalem

PERSIA
(IRAN)

Delhi

ARABIA

Madinah

NILE

Mecca

Ka'bah

GUJARAT

RED
SEA

YEMEN

ARABIAN

SEA

Mogadishu

INDIAN

OCEAN

This is the Dome of the Rock, a beautiful and important Muslim mosque in Jerusalem.

CHAPTER 1

FACTS ABOUT THE ISLAMIC EMPIRES

Welcome to one of the most fascinating civilizations in history, the Islamic Empires. There is a lot to take in because the empires cover such a large portion of the continent of Asia, as well as parts of Africa and Europe. They also span a very long period in history. This section tells you all you need to know about the best and worst times to visit and what the climate and different landscapes are like. It also gives you some important background information about the Muslim way of life and who's who in this vast, exciting world.

WHEN TO VISIT

You will have to get your timing right to see the glories of the Islamic Empires. There was no Islamic world to visit before around 610 CE. This was when the words of **Allah** (God) were first revealed to the **Prophet Muhammad** and the religion of **Islam** began in **Mecca**, in present-day Saudi Arabia. After this, many people converted to Islam. Some **converts** changed to Islam because they thought it was a simpler and better religion. Some were persuaded to become **Muslims** because it often meant paying lower taxes and the chance of getting better schooling and more varied jobs.

EXPANSION

The Islamic world expanded steadily during Muhammad's life and continued to increase in size after the prophet's death in 632 CE. At this time the Islamic world was ruled by religious leaders called **caliphs**. By 640 CE it included what is now Syria, Egypt, Iraq, and Israel. The first major Islamic Empire, called the **Umayyad** Empire, started in 661 CE. The Umayyad Empire expanded rapidly. By 711 CE its caliphs controlled land stretching from western Spain to Afghanistan in the east.

GOLDEN AGE

The best time to visit the Islamic Empires is between 750 and 1258 CE. This period is often known as the Golden Age of Islam. During this period the caliphs' interest in science and knowledge encouraged the spread of new ideas and inventions all over their lands.

Some people were forced to convert to the Islamic religion when Muslim armies attacked and took control of the regions in which they lived.

PEACEFUL CONQUEST

The Islamic Empires were unusually merciful toward people in conquered territories when compared to many other empires. For example, Khalid ibn al-Walid, a 7th-century Muslim general, offered the people of Damascus "security for their lives, prosperity, and churches. Their city walls shall not be demolished, neither shall any Muslim be quartered in their houses. Thereunto we give them the pact of Allah and the protection of his prophet, the caliphs, and the believers. So long as they pay the poll tax, nothing but good shall befall them."

GOOD AND BAD TIMES TO VISIT

610 CE	The Prophet Muhammad turns to the religion of Islam after the Angel Jibril (Gabriel) reveals Allah's truth to him.
622	Muhammad and his followers are chased out of Mecca.
632	Prophet Muhammad dies.
661	Umayyad Empire begins.
750	**Abbasid** Empire begins.
762	Baghdad becomes capital of the Islamic Empires.
750–1258	Era often known as the Golden Age.
800–900	Muhammad's sayings and teachings, called Hadiths, are collected together.
836	Capital of Islamic Empires moves to Samarra, following unrest in Baghdad.
892	Capital returns to Baghdad.
1095–1291	The **Crusades**: Muslims and Christians fight for control of many previously Muslim regions.
1258	**Mongols** attack Baghdad; Abbasid rule comes to an end.

Key:

Stay away	Interesting times to visit	Best times to visit

LANDSCAPE AND CLIMATE

During the Golden Age, the Islamic Empires stretch across many different landscapes, from warm coasts to high, cold mountains. However, most of the empires' lands are in western Asia and North Africa and have a hot, dry, desert climate. It hardly rains here, and you will find deserts full of shifting sand dunes and barren rocks. Because there is little water, very few plants grow, so there is hardly any shade from the burning Sun during the day. Few people live in one place in the desert. Most pass through, resting at scattered **oases**, or water holes, but these are few and far between. If you do not know where you are going, you could risk dying of thirst.

PACK SOMETHING WARM

Travelers to the desert often make the mistake of packing only hot-weather gear. But, because there are no plants to trap the heat at ground level and because dry air cools quickly, a desert can become freezing cold at night. Locals wear animal furs to keep warm, but you may prefer to pack a thick coat. The Sahara in North Africa (below) is the largest desert in the world. Winds here can blow for days at a time, blasting sand and dust into your eyes and face.

RIVERS, MARSHES, AND MOUNTAINS

Many settlements in the Islamic Empires are near permanent water sources. For example, the capital city of the Abbasid Empire, Baghdad, is at the meeting point of two major rivers, the Tigris and Euphrates. The biggest city of the **Fatimid** Empire, Cairo, is on the mighty Nile River. Around the rivers there are fields of crops and groves of date palms and orange trees. Fishermen cast nets from the shore, and trading boats busily sail the waters.

While you are visiting the Islamic Empires, it is also worth going to the huge marshy area south of Baghdad. The Marsh Arabs who live here cut down the abundant reeds growing in the mud and weave them together to make floating villages. See if you can look inside one of their enormous *mudhifs* (village meeting rooms). If you get really sick of the heat, you can climb a mountain in Turkey or Iraq to cool off.

ISLAMIC RELIGION

Wherever you go in the Islamic Empires, you will be aware of the influence of Islam. Religion affects almost every part of a devout (religious) Muslim person's life, so it is useful to know something about the background of Islam before you go.

Muslims believe that the Angel Jibril (Gabriel) came to Earth and passed on a series of **revelations** from Allah (God) to the Prophet Muhammad. When the prophet first told people about this, he gained enemies, and he and his followers were forced out of Mecca to **Madinah** in the north. But gradually Muhammad persuaded others of the truth of Islam. After Muhammad's death in 632 CE, the revelations were remembered and eventually recorded in the **Qur'an**, the Muslim holy book.

PRAYER RITUAL

Muslims are reminded that it is time to pray at the **mosque** by the **muezzin**. He calls out the **Shahadah** from the minaret (high tower) on the mosque. Inside, the **imam** leads the prayers, and all worshippers face in the direction of Mecca.

THE FIVE PILLARS

The Five Pillars are things all devout Muslims should believe or do in their lives. Knowing what these are will give you an insight into some of the aspects of Muslim life you will encounter on your trip.

1. The Shahadah says that you believe in Islam. You will see or hear variations of the phrase "There is no God but Allah and Muhammad is the Messenger of Allah" everywhere you go.

2. One thing you are sure to notice is that the streets are empty of men at midday on Friday. That is because this is a time for prayer for all Muslim males. All Muslims, male and female, pray five times each day, but not always at the mosque.

3. The third pillar is charity, and you will often see Muslims giving money (up to a tenth of their income) to the needy.

4. At **Ramadan** Muslims do not eat or drink for a month during the hours of daylight to recall the time the prophet received the revelations.

5. All Muslims try to make a hajj (**pilgrimage**) to the holy city of Mecca once in their lifetime. Mecca is holy because it is where the prophet received the revelations.

If you are not a Muslim, you do not need to follow the five pillars, and you will still be welcome in the Islamic Empires. The Qur'an teaches that Muslims should be tolerant of people of other religions and places. In the Islamic Empires some people of other religions have high social status.

At Mecca, Muslim pilgrims circle a sacred structure called the Ka'bah. This contains a holy black stone that Muslims believe was sent from heaven to Earth by Allah. ↘

WHO'S WHO IN THE ISLAMIC WORLD?

As a visitor you need to understand the different levels of society in the Islamic Empires. The most important people are the caliphs and **sultans**. Sultans are kings who rule particular areas, and everyone has to treat them with great respect. They live in luxurious homes and surround themselves with trusted bodyguards, tutors, and advisers. Next in line are the **amirs** (military leaders) and then the government officials, such as tax collectors and lawyers.

Merchants and traders are also quite well-to-do and live in very comfortable houses. The majority of ordinary men in the Islamic Empires work as farmers. The lowest-ranking people are those who do lowly or dirty jobs. Below them are slaves, who have been captured from foreign lands.

FAMILY LIFE

Family connections are really important in the Islamic Empires. Different branches of the same family usually live near each other, and several generations often share the same home. Sons and their families generally live with and care for their parents. Daughters often marry second or third cousins and move away. Uncles or cousins often train older boys to do the same jobs that they do, so it is common to have whole families of blacksmiths or soldiers, for instance.

SPECIAL SLAVES

Mamluks are special slaves who are educated and trained to be private soldiers and advisers for caliphs and sultans. These slaves have been captured and brought from distant areas, in order to make sure they have no family links with enemies of the empires. Some mamluks with extraordinary skills became very powerful rulers themselves. For example, Salah ad-Din, the military leader of the Islamic armies in the 11th century, was once a mamluk.

WOMEN AND CHILDREN

What you can do and where you can go in the Islamic Empires depends to a large extent on whether you are male or female. Depending on the family's economic situation, most women spend their days doing household chores or supervising the servants, taking care of children, praying, sewing and doing embroidery, weaving, or playing music. Most girls do not go to school. They learn how to run the home and fetch water from the well or river or to search for fuel for the fire.

Boys might look after herds of animals or work in the fields. Some young boys go to the **madrassah** to learn about their religion. Young boys and girls might play games together, but as they get older, girls stay at home more to keep out of sight of men. This shows that they respect Islamic life. Most girls marry very young—at age 12 or 13.

This family of pilgrims has stopped in the desert on its way to Mecca. The mother and child can be seen in the tent.

Camels are the only reliable means of transportation across the vast desert.

CHAPTER 2

ON THE MOVE

Before you set off on your adventures, there are some bits of practical information you need to know. You can get into real trouble if you wear the wrong clothes or make the wrong gestures. When you are on the move, you may be covering some seriously long distances, so you will need to know the ups and downs of camel travel! Being a tourist in the Islamic Empires can also be hazardous: many people die along the way from thirst, hunger, or overexposure to the Sun.

GETTING AROUND

As a tourist in the Islamic world, you will never get lonely because people are always on the move. Students and scholars travel to Baghdad and other major cities in order to study under great masters. Large armies are constantly on their way to conquer new lands, and **nomads** travel from place to place. And then there are all the pilgrims traveling to and from Mecca.

BY LAND

Many people ride horses or donkeys in the Islamic Empires, but camels are the only animals that can travel long distances across barren land without needing water. Huge camel **caravans**, with lines of up to 2,000 camels, travel across the empires, trading goods such as gold and salt. Ask the locals where the best camel markets are and always hire a guide to travel with you—it is easy to get lost in a desert!

BY SEA

For some journeys you will need to hitch a ride on one of the Muslim trading ships. You will find these **dhows** at new city ports such as Basrah. Dhows carry a crew of 30 or more, so you could work on board to pay for your passage.

This 12th-century map shows the Red Sea and the towns of Madinah (top) and Mecca (bottom). It may look simple, but maps of the Islamic Empires were the best in the world for their time.

Dhows use their huge triangular sails to catch seasonal **monsoon** winds that take them to faraway ports during winter and bring them back in the summer. But sea travel is only for the brave. Ships are made of wooden planks that can be wrecked by storms. And even though Muslims control the seas, there are many pirates waiting to rob and kill those on board.

TRAVEL AIDS

The **astrolabe** is a new invention that you can use to read the positions of the stars and planets to help you navigate. And if you visit after the 14th century, Muslim travelers also use the compass, adopted from the Chinese, to help them find their way around.

TRAVELER'S TIPS

- Bring some snacks! Most travelers eat dried fruits and nuts or olives.
- Bring along a soft cushion for a camel trip. As camels walk their bodies rock and bump from side to side, so you should probably prepare for some motion sickness.
- Camel travel is slow—you will only cover a maximum of about 25 miles (40 kilometers) per day. But a big advantage is that you can use dried camel dung to make campfires to warm you up on cold desert nights!
- It is also a good idea to buy some sweet-smelling frankincense or myrrh to rub under your nose before you set off. They are expensive, but worth it—camels are famous for their bad breath!

WHERE TO STAY

Muslims have a tradition of hospitality and charity. They are very welcoming to pilgrims and travelers, so it should be quite easy for you to find places to stay while traveling through the empires.

IN TOWNS AND CITIES

When you visit towns and cities, you will probably be offered a bed for free in a private home. You might also be able to stay in one of the dormitories that you often find attached to a mosque. These are intended to provide bed and breakfast for weary Muslim pilgrims.

Homes in the Islamic Empires obviously vary in size and style, depending on the wealth of the owner and on where you are in the empires. But a typical Muslim home will be rectangular and surrounded by high walls, with an open courtyard in the middle. Inside there are usually colorful rugs covering the floor and low couches with cushions on which you can lounge.

OUT OF BOUNDS

Homes are separated into men's and women's sections. The women's section is called the **harem**. It is usually at the back and is out of bounds for men. If you wander into the wrong part, you could get yourself into some serious trouble!

The center of this caravanserai courtyard in Turkey has a small oratory, a place where travelers can pray.

IN THE COUNTRYSIDE

Outside the towns and cities, you should look for one of the many **caravanserais** that are scattered across the barren parts of the empires. Rulers ordered these roadside inns to be built to encourage trade. They are each separated by the distance of one day of caravan travel. They allow caravans to stay one or two nights to rest before continuing their journey. Every caravanserai has a large courtyard where you can leave your camels, horses, or donkeys and where animals are given water and food. There are also storage rooms where traders can leave their goods as well as bedrooms for the travelers. Muslim travelers can use the opportunity to pray in a caravanserai, and everyone should take a bath—unless they want to become as smelly as the camels!

In a caravanserai you will get a chance to put your feet up and share travel tips with other tourists, traders, or pilgrims while the animals rest.

WHAT TO WEAR

Even though it is hot in most parts of the Islamic Empires, do not pack your shorts and T-shirts. That would be a surefire way to cause great offense and get yourself into big trouble. People in most parts of the Islamic Empires believe that Allah wants people, especially women, to be modest. All women are expected to cover themselves thoroughly when they are in public, so that men who are not their husbands cannot look at their bodies.

WOMEN'S WEAR

Girls and women should wear a long, loose robe that covers their ankles. Alternatively they should wear a loose tunic that goes below the knees and a pair of baggy pants to go underneath this. Make sure you get them made of cotton or linen, because these fabrics are cool and good at absorbing sweat. Do not forget to buy a matching veil as well. To fit in, you will need to pull the veil across your face when you are out and about, but you can loosen it again when you are inside.

This woman's costume is typical of the clothes worn by girls and women in the Islamic Empires.

BE SAFE IN THE SUN

Sunblock is not available yet, so wearing long, loose clothes is the only way to prevent sunburn. Wear white or light-colored robes because these reflect (rather than absorb) the heat and will help to keep you cool. In the desert wear a scarf around your head, like the locals, to stop sand from blowing into your eyes and mouth.

MEN'S FASHION TIPS

Men should wear long, loose shirts and baggy pants, too, but get your tunic hemmed carefully, because Muslims in the empires believed you could end up in hell if your tunic was too long. They also wear a long piece of cloth as a sort of cloak. This can double as both a sunshade and an umbrella, depending on the weather. In some places men wear a turban, a long piece of cloth wound tightly around the head that also protects them from the desert sand and Sun. Many Arab men are proud of their turbans, and it is considered a great insult to knock off another man's turban!

Finally, the Qur'an tells men they should not wear silk clothes or gold jewelry. If you do, people will think you are a big show-off who is bragging about his wealth, and you will not be welcome anywhere.

This man is wearing the long tunic and turban favored by most men during the Golden Age of the Islamic Empires.

FOOD AND DRINK

The food you will be offered in the Islamic Empires will vary from place to place, but generally it will be healthy and delicious. There are figs and oranges, olives, dishes made with eggplant, and flat breads and grains. Sheep's milk and goat's milk are used to make yogurt and feta cheese. Dessert lovers can get sweet pastries made with sugar, honey, nuts, eggs, and dried fruit. Spicy foods are made using flavorings such as cinnamon, cumin, and cloves, which are bought and sold by traders. But watch out because there are no refrigerators, and spices often disguise the taste of food that has gone bad!

FEAST OR FAMINE?

You should find plenty to eat on your travels. Muslim farmers use dung and other fertilizers to help grow healthy crops. They also build canals and water wheels to channel or collect water to **irrigate** their dry lands. But you will go hungry if you arrive in an area that has just been hit by a plague of locusts. A swarm of these grasshopper-like insects can destroy a field of grain in hours, a fact that earns them a mention in the Qur'an.

Many markets in the Islamic Empires have colorful, strong-smelling spices for sale. Just follow your nose and you will find them! ➤

MEATY MEALS

For those of you who cannot last a week without ham or bacon, here is the bad news: the eating of pork is forbidden, partly because pigs are considered unclean animals. But you can eat meat from other animals as long as it is **halal**, which means the animals have been slaughtered humanely. Islamic law says that people should be kind to all Allah's creatures, so animals have their throats slit to cause them minimum suffering. Camel and goat meat are two local delicacies you might like to try.

Here, cooks knead bread and stir bubbling cauldrons of meat over open fires in preparation for a large meal.

ELEPHANT MEAT

Muslims are also discouraged from eating elephant meat. If you ask why, you may get to hear an old legend about a **sheikh** and 30 men who got lost on a mountain. Even though the sheikh told them not to, the hungry men killed and ate a small elephant. That night elephants killed all the men, but carried the sheikh safely back to a village.

DRINKS

You will not go thirsty in the cities. To fulfil their promise to donate to charity (the fourth pillar of Islam), wealthy Muslims build public drinking fountains from which everyone can get fresh drinking water. And when you arrive at people's houses, the first thing they will do is offer you a drink—perhaps a sweet mint tea or even juice made from sugary lemon syrup.

CUSTOMS AND BELIEFS

Some of the most important Muslim customs are connected with mosques. At the door, all worshippers must take off their shoes and wash in a fountain or pool there. This ritual washing is called *wudu*, and it symbolizes people wanting to make themselves pure and clean before worshipping Allah.

Inside, all the male worshippers sit on the floor as a sign that they are all considered equal by Allah. When women come to the mosque, they always have their heads covered and sit in a different part, but often they will pray at home instead.

Modern Muslims wash before entering a mosque, just as Muslims have always done.

MARRIAGE CUSTOMS

The Islamic world at this time is not the place to look for a vacation romance. It is not the custom for young people to go on dates, since marriages are arranged by parents. The bride and groom often do not meet until their wedding day. Try to go to a Muslim wedding if you get the chance. The bride usually travels to the groom's house in a closed tent on a camel's back.

She is accompanied by musicians and men carrying gifts and her **dowry** (money from her family). The wedding celebrations usually go on for days, with music, singing, and fine foods.

FESTIVAL CUSTOMS

Muslim festivals are serious religious occasions, but they are also public holidays. For example, after the month of fasting for Ramadan, Muslims gather together for Eid al Fitr, a three-day celebration during which they dress up in new clothes, enjoy feasting, and give each other gifts.

The end of Ramadan is a great cause for celebration across the Islamic Empires.

MIND YOUR MANNERS!

Table manners are considered very important in the Islamic Empires.

- At mealtimes you must always wash your hands before sitting down on the floor on a rug or small pillow.
- When seated, never point the soles of your feet toward another person. This is a great insult because feet are considered dirty.
- There are no knives and forks. You will be expected to eat using your right hand only.
- When you meet someone new, you must also remember to shake with your right hand because it would be a great insult to use the left. People in the Islamic Empires use their left hand for washing. (There is no toilet paper in the Islamic Empires, so you have to use soap and water instead.)

The remarkable spiral minaret of the Great Mosque at Samarra is a must-see for sightseers visiting the Islamic Empires.

CHAPTER 3

SIGHTSEEING

There are some top attractions in the Islamic Empires that everyone should see. The palaces are decorated with gold and precious materials, and the mosques are places of great beauty and peace. And in the huge, newly built city of Baghdad you can visit zoos, museums, and gardens and try some of the most delicious food in the world. But make sure you visit at the right time, or you could find yourself dodging arrows and severed heads!

BAGHDAD

For a weekend city break, Baghdad is definitely the place to go. Completed in 762 CE, it took 100,000 architects, craftsmen, and workers from all over the Islamic world to build. But be careful not to visit between 836 and 892 CE. During this time the caliph moved his court to Samarra, and warring rulers caused great trouble in the city. At one stage, rocks, severed heads from enemy warriors, and flaming pots of oil rained down on Baghdad, all shot from catapults outside the city gates!

Get your camera ready! Ancient Baghdad is bursting with beautiful buildings such as this tomb of the wife of a 9th-century caliph.

CIRCULAR CITY

You can get your bearings in Baghdad in a day because it was designed as two circles, one inside the other, with the outer one about 1 mile (2 kilometers) in diameter. Roads run outward toward all parts of the Islamic world.

Baghdad is a rich, colorful place, with mosques, museums, zoos, and libraries. Cooks here are famous for their elaborate dishes. Typical sweets include halvah (made from sesame seeds) and baklava (made from pastry, spices, and chopped nuts).

A TOUR OF THE CITY

Follow these directions for an interesting tour of the city:

1. Start on the outskirts and follow the busy markets to the moat. Pass through one of the four gates in the double-brick outer city walls. The crowded streets inside are packed with small houses, where the poorer people live.

2. Toward the center you should see a green dome with the figure of a rider holding a spear on top of the caliph's palace. The wider streets here are lined with shops and large merchants' houses. At the famous House of Wisdom you can see scholars discussing new ideas and inventions. Try asking them to turn lead coins into gold . . .

3. When you reach the second set of city walls, it could take a while to get past the guards at the gate. They check visitors carefully, but it is worth the wait. Inside is the heart of the city, with the government buildings, grand mosque, and sumptuous royal palace.

FROM LEAD TO GOLD

Some Arabic scholars at this time believed that any metal could be changed into gold or silver if they could discover a rare substance, known as *al-iksir* (hence the English word *elixir*), a red powder made from a legendary "philosopher's stone."

PALACES AND FORTRESSES

The other must-see buildings are the palaces. These huge constructions are designed to show off the power of the sultans, caliphs, princes, and amirs who live in them. They are often built like castles to keep out enemy forces.

A typical grand palace usually contains a maze-like sequence of rooms. These include a private mosque or place for prayer and separate living quarters for the owner, his family, his many wives, servants, advisers, and soldiers and their horses. The palace often has its own water and food supplies so that people inside can remain self-sufficient during a siege.

SHOWING OFF WEALTH

Rulers like to show off their wealth, so they fill their palaces with rare items from the far corners of the Islamic world. Rooms are often lined with imported stone such as marble and jade, rare woods, and finely woven wall hangings. If you get a chance to go into a palace, do not be insulted by the servants. They will try to sprinkle you with rosewater so that your smell does not offend the delicate royal noses!

Get away from the heat by wandering among the shady plants in the gardens. You will also enjoy the soothing sound of the fountains, although your peace may be interrupted by strange noises. Many of the wealthiest rulers have zoos in their palaces that are stocked with exotic animals, such as zebras, from across the empires.

THE HALL OF THE TREE
At the sultan's palace in Baghdad, ask if you can see the Hall of the Tree. This is a special room the caliph had made to keep him amused. It contains a huge artificial tree that is made entirely of gold and silver and filled with gold mechanical birds that chirp.

THE CITADEL OF ALEPPO

There are fortresses dotted all over the empires to make sure Islamic forces are not overthrown. There are lots to visit, but one of the best is the Citadel of Aleppo in Syria. The only way in is over a narrow bridge across the wide moat and through a series of three iron doors. Beyond this is a dark, twisting entrance passage with slit windows high above it. Glance up to check that soldiers are not preparing to pour boiling oil on to you, mistaking you for an enemy!

You cannot miss the enormous citadel in Aleppo, built high on a hill overlooking the flat lands all around.

MOSTLY MOSQUES

Follow in the footsteps of Muhammad and visit some of the holiest places in the Islamic Empires, where the prophet spent his life. Apart from the **Ka'bah**, in Mecca, you should try to visit the mosque in nearby Madinah. Its shape is based on the prophet's house, which was built around an open, square, walled courtyard. When it was first constructed, the mosque building had simple mud walls, but successive empires redecorated it with marble and other expensive materials. The prophet is buried under the stone floor.

THE DOME OF THE ROCK

From Madinah, it is a long, hot journey to Jerusalem to see the Dome of the Rock. This is a beautiful octagonal building with a golden dome on top. Inside is a rock, but not just any rock. This is where Muslims believe Muhammad went up to Allah in heaven. It was originally a Jewish temple. The rock is also important to Jews, who believe it symbolizes the foundation stone upon which the world was built.

HOW ARE MOSQUES USED?

This checklist will help you figure out what's what in a mosque:

Minaret: Most mosques have towers called minarets that the muezzin climbs to call in all directions.

Mihrab: A niche (hollow) in the wall reminds worshippers which way Mecca is.

Minbar: The imam leads communal prayer or delivers a sermon from this raised seat or platform with steps leading to it.

Mosques are sacred buildings that have to be big enough to accommodate lots of worshippers. Mosques are also centers for the Islamic community. There are many separate rooms around the courtyards. Some rooms are used as madrassahs (religious schools) where people come to learn about the Qur'an. The courtyards themselves are often used for political and social purposes, such as concerts of religious music or the recruitment of soldiers.

THE GREAT MOSQUE AT CORDOBA

When the Abbasid Empire replaced the Umayyad Empire in 750 CE, an Umayyad prince named Abd al-Rahman moved to Spain and created a new outpost of the Islamic world. Cordoba was its capital, and the Great Mosque was its jewel. Plain on the outside, the interior is a huge hall with a roof supported high up by striped double arches resting on stone columns. The arched shapes look rather like palm trees, the trunks of which supported the roof on Muhammad's home.

You will feel small in the Great Mosque of Cordoba. It was built to be large enough for all Muslims in the city to meet in prayer.

DECORATIVE DESIGNS

You will soon notice that many Islamic buildings, especially mosques and palaces, and also objects such as plates, books, and bowls, are decorated with writing. This beautiful writing is called **calligraphy**.

The best calligraphers in the Islamic Empires, such as the 11th-century master Ibn al-Bawwab, devote their lives to the art. They become so famous that they get to write just for the rich and powerful. Their tools are hand-cut reed pens, fine papers, and specially prepared inks. To decorate large surfaces on buildings, skilled masons carve calligraphy directly into stone or brick, and builders use cement to position tiles painted with words.

Here are some excellent places to spot beautiful calligraphy:
- around the top of the Dome of the Rock (see top right of picture, opposite)
- on the Friday Mosque in Isfahan, Iran
- in the public libraries.

See if you can find examples of calligraphy in which the letters of a word are drawn in special shapes so they look like animals.

I-SPY PATTERNS

On buildings throughout the Islamic Empires, there are lots of geometric patterns to look out for. There are regular shapes, such as squares, rectangles, circles, pentagons, and triangles, that are repeated and linked together in interesting ways. In Islam these patterns represent the order and infinite power of Allah. Some shapes have special meanings. For example, stars represent the spreading of the Islamic world in all directions from the center. They have 5, 6, 8, 10, 12, or even 16 points and are designed by dividing a circle into equal parts.

IMAGE-FREE ZONE

You will not see pictures or models of people on mosques. This is rather different from European churches, where there are statues and paintings of saints. This tradition comes from the belief of many Muslims that, since Allah created people and animals, it is disrespectful for humans to try to recreate them. Other Muslims do think it is acceptable to make paintings of great rulers or military leaders or of life in the Islamic Empires. But these mostly appear as illustrations in non-religious books and are therefore small and very detailed.

Glazed tiles are used to add color and make Islamic buildings weatherproof.

Beautiful rugs and carpets are on sale in many bazaars in the Islamic Empires.

CHAPTER 4

THINGS TO DO

There is plenty to keep you busy in the Islamic
Empires besides sightseeing. You can borrow a
horse and try to score a goal in a fast, furious
polo game. If you are feeling brave (and strong)
you could try your luck in a sweaty wrestling
match. After a tiring day's shopping and bargaining
in the bustling bazaars, there are many ways to
relax. Pull up a cushion with the locals for a game
of chess, listen to a talented musician, or marvel
at a storyteller's accounts of great battles and
faraway places.

SPORTS AND GAMES

Young men in the Islamic Empires are encouraged to take part in sports to become strong and competitive. This will make them good business leaders and warriors. But, like many things in the Islamic Empires, what you get to do might depend on who you know. Caliphs, courtiers, and wealthy men do archery, go hunting with falcons, or go horse racing and play polo. Ordinary people do not have the time or money to do these things, but they might watch cock fights and ram fights.

RACING AND POLO

Racing—including horse racing, boat racing, and even camel racing—is probably the most popular sport. The sleek Arabian horse is extremely fast. Horse racing is excellent for training cavalry officers because battles often take place between armies on horseback, with archers shooting as they ride. Polo is an Islamic invention and is also good for riding skills. It is a bit like hockey on horseback.

In polo, two teams of riders compete to knock a wooden ball into a goal using a long wooden mallet.

PLAYING CHESS

Chess is all the rage in the Islamic Empires. The Arabs learned to play chess from the Sassanids when they conquered them and took over the Persian Empire in 651 CE. The Persians probably learned it from the Indians, and the Indians themselves probably learned a version of it from the Chinese. After the Arabs took over Spain, chess gradually passed on to Europe, too.

MUSIC AND STORYTELLING

Music and storytelling are very popular throughout the Islamic Empires. Some of the musical entertainment you will hear is religious. Praise-songs, which literally sing the praises of the Prophet Muhammad, began after his death, and you will often hear Islamic chanting during Ramadan.

Caliphs pay musicians and dancers to entertain them at court, and female slaves are often trained to play music for the sultans. Favorite instruments include the lute, a four-stringed instrument called the oud, the tambourine-like riq, finger cymbals, drums made of clay with goatskin, and the ney (a long cane flute).

Several musicians can be seen here playing drums and other instruments at a royal wedding.

Across the Islamic Empires, many local folk music and dance traditions continued after the people became Muslims. For example, the **Bedouin** nomads still sing and dance the ancient songs of the desert. Some folk dances celebrate warriors' achievements, such as the Arabian sword dance; others celebrate the harvests or the changing seasons. You will also see some folk singers performing for money on the streets.

ENTERTAINMENT RULES

In many parts of the Islamic Empires, dancing is allowed and enjoyed. But do not get carried away by the music and ask for a dancing partner. Men and women are not allowed to dance together.

STORIES AND BOOKS

On the streets and in dining halls in some towns and cities, poets and storytellers entertain people with exotic tales full of excitement and romance. Thanks to Muslim scholars, you can also buy your own books. Muslims learned how to make paper from Chinese papermakers. Paper soon replaced parchment (animal hides) and papyrus (made from reed plants) because it could be made virtually anywhere from rags and waste fibers.

Islamic libraries have hundreds of thousands of books, compared to the small libraries in **monasteries** and universities in the West at this time. There are more than 100 paper stores and bookstores in Papersellers' Street near the main mosque in Baghdad.

The sword dance, seen here being performed in Saudi Arabia, has not changed over the centuries.

ARABIAN NIGHTS

If you are looking for a book to keep you amused on your journey, pick up a copy of *The Arabian Nights*. This book tells the story of Scheherazade, a beautiful queen who tells her cruel new husband stories every night for 1,001 nights. She always finishes on a cliff-hanger so he will not kill her in the morning, as he had done to many wives before. Finally, she cures him of his murderous habit. The book is full of colorful characters such as Aladdin, Sinbad, and Ali Baba and the 40 thieves.

SHOPPING

If you like to shop until you drop, then you have come to the right place at the right time! The **bazaars** of the Islamic Empires are packed with beautiful things to tempt you. But first make sure you have the right **currency**.

For large purchases you will need dinars (coins made with gold brought from Africa). Smaller coins include the silver dirhem and the copper fals. Most are beautifully decorated with verses from the Qur'an. And if you leave your wallet at home, some merchants will let you buy goods with an order of payment, which works like a modern check.

The coins of the Islamic Empires are marked with their name, the place they were minted (or made), and the year they were made.

PRAYER MATS AND WOVEN GOODS

There is a great tradition of weaving rugs and blankets here. Nomads need rugs and cushions, which they sit on in their tents, to be easy to pack up when they move from place to place. Prayer mats are designed for one person to kneel and pray on. There is often a colorful pattern pointing toward the top of the prayer mat so that Muslims can place the rug facing toward Mecca when they pray.

A BRAYING SHOPPING CART

There are so many souvenirs to choose from, you might end up buying quite a lot from Muslim bazaars. How will you get all your purchases home? Rent a donkey, as the locals do. In the Islamic Empires, donkeys are "beasts of burden" and are used to carry heavy loads over short distances.

JEWELRY, POTTERY, AND PAINTINGS

The jewelry worn by the nomads makes a beautiful gift. You can get earrings, necklaces, belts, ankle and hand decorations, and even nose rings made out of silver in the Middle East. You can also pick up beautiful bronze, copper, brass, silver, and gold objects.

This little 10th-century deer from Cordoba would make an unusual ornament.

Some stalls offer pottery tiles, dishes, or pots often decorated with calligraphy and swirling or geometric designs. The king and his family get all the best pieces, but you should still find some good souvenirs. If you have the time and money, why not have a miniature portrait painted? Miniature paintings are very fashionable. You could even have yourself drawn as part of a lavish court or heroic battle scene, as many of the rulers do.

The 13th-century Great Mosque of Divrigi, in Turkey, also served as a hospital and medical school.

CHAPTER 5

HEALTH AND SAFETY

Before you take a trip anywhere during this period, remember to get your innoculations (shots) up to date. There are many fatal diseases in the Islamic Empires that we no longer have to worry about today, such as smallpox. You should be safe most of the time, partly because caliphs keep roads safe for travelers so that Muslims can travel to Mecca freely. But this is also a violent time, and you may find yourself in danger if you do not know the rules.

HEALTH AND HYGIENE

There is no excuse for not keeping clean and smelling sweet while you are on vacation in the Islamic Empires. One of the prophet's teachings is the importance of keeping your body clean. This makes the Islamic Empires cleaner and healthier than most other parts of the world at this time. Most houses have drains to take away dirty water, and every town has at least one if not several **hammams** (public bathhouses). They are open from early in the morning until late at night. They are also cheap to visit, so everyone can afford to bathe regularly.

This shows a bathhouse. ↘

TIME FOR TEETH

If you forget to pack a toothbrush, use a miswak stick and sweeten your breath with herbs and spices, as the locals do. Dentists here will pull out bad teeth and can also make you a false set, if you do not mind them being made out of bone!

men's baths

disrobing hall

cool room

hot room

furnace

women's baths

VISITING A HAMMAM

Here are a few things you need to know before you go:

- Hammams have separate sections for men and women, or men and women visit at separate times of day. Check this before you enter.
- In the women-only section you can strip off all your clothes, but the men are expected to wear towels around their waists.
- You are only allowed to visit the barber if you have not eaten garlic, since this is considered very impolite and unfair to him!
- There are usually three rooms. The hot room generally has a large domed ceiling and a marble slab where you can get a massage. The warm room is for washing, and the cool room is where you go to relax and drink tea.

Hammams are not just places to wash. You can also catch up on local news and gossip, meet people, relax, drink tea, and even get a haircut and a massage.

HYGIENE POLICE

In Islamic cities the Muhtasib (public service inspectors) enforce strict hygiene regulations. They check restaurants, butchers, and slaughterhouses to see that the hygiene rules are being followed, and anyone caught selling rotten meat is executed. They also check the quality of the water in hammams and ensure that people obey the rules and do not dump their garbage on the streets. At this time few people in Europe even have access to clean drinking water, regular baths, or a sewage system!

DOCTORS AND HOSPITALS

If, after all your attempts to keep clean and avoid illness, you do need to see a doctor, you have come to the right place. Muslim doctors are very advanced, and their invention of hospital wards has saved thousands of lives. If you get sick in some other parts of the world at this time, you could find yourself sharing a pus-covered, flea-infested bed with five other people (some of whom might already be dead)! In the Islamic Empires you will be treated in good hospitals by skilled practitioners who understand the importance of hygiene.

HOSPITAL CARE

Sultans and caliphs have built fine hospitals across many parts of the Islamic world. These treat anyone for free and are open 7 days a week and 24 hours a day. They have separate blocks for men and women and separate wards for people with different diseases, in order to limit the spread of disease. Each hospital has staff members who specialize in different fields of medicine, from surgeons to bone setters. And there is no need to worry if you get sick out of town—one of the latest mobile hospitals should come along soon. Medical teams on horseback, fully equipped with medicines and medical instruments, set up tents in remote villages to treat patients. They also follow armies into battle.

DOCTORS AND DISEASE

Doctors in the Islamic Empires came up with the idea that disease was caused and spread by the tiny organisms we call germs today. If you happen to be in Baghdad around 900 CE you will see something very odd! This is when Doctor al-Razi famously chose the site for a new hospital in Baghdad by hanging pieces of meat in different parts of the city and examined them to see which took the longest time to rot. This made him the first doctor to link food decay with the quality of air in a place and to link that with the possible spread of infection.

BLOODLETTING

In spite of many huge medical advances, Muslim practitioners, like many doctors in Europe at this time, also use bloodletting (or "cupping") to draw inflammation to the surface of the body or to take away aches and pains. A cut is made in the skin (often on the patient's back) and a cup put over the area to create suction to pull out a small amount of blood. Yuck!

While patients in other countries have to bite down on a stick to endure the pain of an operation, Islamic doctors have invented anesthetics that allow their patients to sleep through it! They give patients substances such as opium or lettuce seed to knock them out.

If you got sick 1,000 years ago, your best bet for survival was to get an appointment with one of the highly trained doctors of the Islamic Empires.

KEEPING SAFE

Even though wars are common and life can be pretty violent, the age of the Islamic Empires is a safer time to travel than ever before. Before Islam, nomadic tribes would frequently rob and kill travelers. Muhammad and later Islamic leaders introduced laws to bring order to the empires. The caliph's officials would enforce some pretty stern punishments if these laws were disobeyed.

Here is a list of some typical punishments for law breakers that you might see being carried out on the streets.
- Adultery: Death by stoning
- Highway robbery: Execution, or right hand and left foot cut off
- Theft: Right hand cut off (second offense: Left foot cut off)
- Drinking alcohol: Eighty lashes with a whip.

DANGEROUS WORDS

Remember to watch your language. A slip of the tongue will be harshly punished. If a caliph objects to something you say, a simple wave of his hand can tell the executioner to put you to death immediately. And be careful what you write in letters home while on vacation. The caliphs have networks of spies to make sure everyone in the empires lives by their rules. Ibn Muqla was an important calligrapher who had his right hand cut off for writing something rude about a caliph.

THE EVIL EYE

If you still do not feel safe, invest in a charm to ward off evil. Many Muslims at this time, especially in North Africa, believe that certain people can spread bad luck through their eyes. To prevent the evil eye, you can buy magical objects such as "the hand of Fatimah" or raise your left hand in protection. So, remember not to hold up your left hand as a greeting, or people might take offense.

Here, a vizier (official of the Muslim court) watches as a criminal is executed.

DHIMMIES

If you are not a Muslim, one way of ensuring safe passage through the Islamic Empires is to become a dhimmie. Dhimmies are people who do not want to become Muslims but do want to be part of the Islamic Empires, so they pay a tax to the ruler. By doing so they become dhimmies, which means "protected people." In this way they gain the same rights as Muslims as well as the protection of the Islamic government.

HEADS OFF!

If you want to keep your head, never say anything that might be understood as blasphemous (an insult to Allah or Islam). This is the worst sin you could commit in the Islamic Empires, and it is punishable by death.

Decorative mosaics adorn a wall inside the Friday Mosque in Iran. The building is now a museum that houses examples of Islamic architecture dating back to the 11th century.

CHAPTER 6

USEFUL INFORMATION

This is an easy reference guide for the time traveler visiting the Islamic Empires. First, there is a phrase book to help you read the beautiful Arabic script and a numbers guide to help you understand how much everything is going to cost you. There is also a brief history section to explain what brought about the end of the Golden Age of the Islamic Empires and to warn you about some of the bloody battles that caused its downfall. Finally, there is a timeline so you can check at a glance what times you need to visit in order to see particular events or people.

GETTING TO KNOW ARABIC

A	أ
B	ب
T	ت
TH	ث
J	ج
H	ح
KH	خ
D	د
Z or DH	ذ
R	ر
Z	ز
S	س
SH	ش
S	ص
D	ض
T	ط
DH or Z	ظ
' or 3	ع
GH	غ
F	ف
Q	ق
K	ك
L	ل
M	م
N	ن
H	ه
W or U	و
Y or i	ي

The Arabic language started as a dialect used by nomads in the Arabian deserts. The spread of the words of the Qur'an took Arabic across the Islamic world. Caliphs and other rulers and their administrators encouraged the use of one written form of the language so that they could control their empires. With a little Arabic, everyone can understand each other, even though they might also speak other languages. Why not try learning a bit of Arabic yourself?

USEFUL PHRASES

Here are some useful words and phrases, written as you say them in Arabic (not in Arabic symbols).

English	Arabic pronunciation
Peace be upon you	As-salaamu 'aleykum
And upon you be peace . . .	Wa 'aleykum as-salaam
My name is . . .	Ana ismi . . .
What is your name?	Matha ismuka . . .
I want to buy . . .	Ana ureed an ashtiree . . .
I want to visit . . .	Ana ureed an azoor . . .
I speak English	Ana Atakallum al- Injileeziya
How much?	Bikam?
That's expensive	Hatha ghaalee
Until we meet again	ila al-Liqa'

The Arabic alphabet has 28 symbols representing sounds and words. The symbols are written and read from right to left.

This says "As-salaamu 'aleykum," which means, "Peace be upon you." Try writing it yourself in Arabic. The arrows tell you in which direction you should move your pencil.

STANDARD NUMBERS

At the start of the Islamic Empires, people figured out sums in many different ways. Many merchants and traders counted on their fingers and wrote numbers in words. Others used letters of the alphabet to mean numbers. Using letters of the alphabet, the first nine letters represent 1 to 9; the next nine letters represent 10 to 90; the next nine 100 to 900; and z, the last letter, is 1,000. However, in the 8th century, travelers brought back a newer system of writing the numbers 1 to 9 using symbols from India. The symbols changed slightly as people accepted the system and learned to write them. This was not easy because, unlike letters, the numbers are written from left to right.

Eventually a standard form of Arabic numbers was used not only throughout the Islamic Empires, but also in Europe and other parts of the world. This was very important because it made international trade much easier.

You will definitely recognize most of the numbers, but beware: depending on when you go, 2 and 3 might be on their sides and 4 and 5 look very unusual.

1	2	3	4	5	6	7	8	9	10	from 11th century

1	2	3	4	5	6	7	8	9	from 14th century

END OF THE GOLDEN AGE

What should you expect to see if you arrive in the regions of the Islamic Empires after the end of its so-called Golden Age? The Abbasid caliphs are the last rulers of the Golden Age. By the 12th century their rule is becoming weaker, as bickering over religious differences worsens and some rulers are assassinated.

THE CRUSADES

The Islamic Empires are further weakened by the Crusades. These military campaigns from 1095 to 1291 CE were also known as holy wars. They were fought by Christian knights who wanted to take the holy city of Jerusalem back from the Muslims and to help the Christian emperor of Constantinople in his wars against Muslim Turks. The battles continued for 200 years, as Christians tried to get rid of Muslims from a far wider area, including Spain. By 1100 the crusaders had claimed Jerusalem, and it was ruled by a Christian king. But in 1187 Islamic leader and Egyptian sultan Salah al-Din won back the city. However, by 1291 many Muslim strongholds had fallen to the Christians, and the Islamic military forces were badly weakened.

MONGOL ATTACK

The final straw came in 1258, when Baghdad was attacked and destroyed by the Mongols. This was the first time the Muslim world was overrun by non-Muslims. The Mongols left a trail of death and destruction from which the Abbasid Empire never recovered. Trade routes became unsafe and law and order broke down. The Golden Age had ended.

BATTLE SCENES

If you have a strong stomach, you could drop in on one of the battles during the Crusades. These were bloody affairs, and at one point the streets of Jerusalem were said to be ankle-deep with blood. Weapons used included siege machines that battered down gates, bows and arrows, spears and swords, flame throwers, and even exploding grenades.

LATER EMPIRES

If you want to see the Islamic Empires after the Golden Age, there are still some fascinating places to visit. For example, the Mongol emperor who conquered Baghdad converted to Islam, and ancestors of his who conquered India went on to rule the great Mughal Empire from 1526 until 1857. The Muslim Safavid Empire that ruled Iran from 1501 until 1736 is also worth a visit, especially if you stop over to see their elegant capital, Isfahan. And the Ottomans, a dynasty of Turkish sultans who ruled much of the Mediterranean and the Middle East from the 14th century to the early 20th century, are known for their strict rule, sumptuous clothing, and beautiful tiled palaces and mosques.

THE FALL OF BAGHDAD

If you do risk traveling to see the fall of Baghdad, you will be horrified by the change in the city. Two million Muslims are killed in the attack, and many mosques, hospitals, schools, and even roads and waterways are destroyed. So many books from the House of Wisdom are dumped in the Euphrates River that their ink turns its waters black.

Built in 1617, the Blue Mosque in Turkey has 260 windows that keep it well lit in daytime.

THE ISLAMIC EMPIRES AT A GLANCE

TIMELINE

570 CE	Birth of Muhammad.
610	Muhammad receives first messages from the Angel Jibril (Gabriel).
622	The **hijrah** (when Muhammad and his followers were forced out of Mecca and moved to Madinah).
632	Death of Muhammad. Abu Bakr becomes the first caliph.
634	Abu Bakr dies and Umar becomes caliph.
634–644	Muslim armies invade Syria, Egypt, and Iraq.
638	Muslim soldiers take Jerusalem.
644	Umar is assassinated and Uthman becomes caliph.
644–650	Muslim armies invade Iran and Afghanistan and enter North Africa.
656	Uthman is assassinated and Ali becomes caliph.
661	Ali is assassinated and the new caliph, Muawiya, is the first ruler of the Umayyad dynasty.
685	In Jerusalem work starts on the building of the Dome of the Rock.
705	The Great Mosque in Damascus is built.
750	The Abbasids take over from the Umayyads as rulers of the Islamic Empires.
762	Baghdad becomes capital of the Islamic Empires.
784	Work starts on the great Mosque of Cordoba, in Spain.
836	Capital of Islamic Empires moves to Samarra.
892	Capital of Islamic Empires moves back to Baghdad.
969	Fatimids defeat Abbasids in Egypt.
973	Fatimid rulers make Cairo, in Egypt, the Islamic Empires' capital.

1206	Mongol tribes unite under new leader Chinghis (Genghis) Khan.
1258	Mongols attack Baghdad and Abbasid rule over the Islamic Empires comes to an end.
1380s–1405	Mongol leader Timur conquers much of central Asia, Iran, and Iraq.
1453	Ottomans capture Constantinople, in what is now Turkey, and rename it Istanbul.
1492	Christians achieve complete control of Spain.
1501	The Safavids found their empire in Iran.
1520–1566	The period of rule by Ottoman sultan Suleiman the Magnificent.
1556–1605	The period of rule of the first Mughal emperor in India, Akbar the Great.
1628–1658	Rule of famous Mughal emperor Shah Jahan, who built the Taj Mahal.

FURTHER READING

BOOKS

Barber, Nicola. *History in Art: Islamic Empires*. Chicago: Raintree, 2005.

Corzine, Phyllis. *World History: The Islamic Empire*. San Diego: Lucent, 2004.

Doak, Robin. *Great Empires of the Past: Empire of the Islamic World*. New York: Facts on File, 2004.

WEBSITES

- www.pbs.org/empires/islam
  Click on "Educational resources" for many interesting articles about faith and culture in the Islamic Empires.

- www.historyforkids.org/learn/islam/history
  Click on these links to learn more about the Islamic Empires.

GLOSSARY

Abbasid dynasty of caliphs and other leaders who ruled the second Islamic Empire from 750 to 1258 CE

Allah Arabic word for God

amir military leader

astrolabe instrument used by sailors to read the positions of the stars and planets when navigating

bazaar open-air market with shops and stalls for selling goods

Bedouin tribe of nomadic desert people from the Middle East and North Africa

caliph civil and religious ruler of a Muslim state or empire

calligraphy art of beautiful writing, especially in religious works

caravan long line of camels that travels across the Islamic Empires

caravanserai roadside inn where travelers can rest

convert someone who changes religion

crusade holy war

currency money or unit of exchange for goods or services

dhow ship with large triangular sails, used for trading

dowry gift of money or valuables made by a bride's family to a groom's family when the couple gets married

Fatimid dynasty of caliphs and other leaders who ruled an Islamic empire based in Cairo from 909 to 1171 CE

halal Islamic religious food preparation laws

hammam public bathhouse

harem women's quarters in a Muslim palace or home

hijrah Muhammad's emigration with his followers from Mecca to Madinah in 622 CE

imam person who leads prayers in mosque

irrigate water crops in fields

Islam religion based on the word of Allah, received by the Prophet Muhammad, and on Muhammad's teachings

Ka'bah square building in Mecca believed by Muslims to be the house Ibrahim erected for God and the focus of Muslim worship

Madinah city in Saudi Arabia where Muhammad lived after he became prophet; also known as Medina

madrassah religious school linked to a mosque

Mecca holiest Muslim city

monastery place where a strict religious community lives

Mongols tribe of nomadic people from Mongolia, in central Asia

monsoon season of very wet weather caused by moist winds blowing on to Asia from the Indian Ocean

mosque place of Muslim worship

muezzin man who calls Muslim worshippers to prayer

Muhammad founder of Islam, also known as the Prophet of God

Muslim person who believes in Islam

nomad member of ethnic group with no permanent home who moves animals between grazing places

oasis small area in the desert watered by springs and wells

observatory building from which people can study the stars

pilgrimage journey to a sacred place or shrine

prophet someone who hears and passes on the word of God

Qur'an sacred book of Islam

Ramadan month of fasting during hours of daylight

revelations God's word as passed on to people

Shahadah first pillar of Islam—the statement "There is no god but Allah, and Muhammad is his prophet"

sheikh Arab chief or prince

sultan king in the Islamic Empires

Umayyad dynasty of caliphs and other leaders who ruled the first Islamic Empire from 661 to 750 CE

INDEX